A Special Gift

Presented to _____

From _____

Date _____

Published by C.R. Gibson®

C.R. Gibson® is a registered trademark of Thomas Nelson, Inc.,
Nashville, Tennessee 37214

Art Direction by Joel Anderson
Illustration and Design by Kristi Carter Smith
Anderson Thomas Design, Nashville, Tennessee

Written and developed by Matthew A. Price

Printed in Mexico

GB107

ISBN 0-7667-8191-7

UPC 0-82272-47841-1

Once Upon A Time...

There was a bang.

A **big** bang...

An explosion of creation

so great that within moments
energy erupted with such

white-hot intensity

that the basic subatomic elements
— electrons, neutrons, and protons —
were instantaneously formed.

Soon gravitational forces squeezed and heated these first atoms until gradually the universe began to fill up with a **soupy mix** of hydrogen, helium, ice, and dust. Time passed . . .

Gravity continued to cook the whole **swirling mass** until pieces of floating matter eventually **formed into stars —** — including our **Sun,** which became the hub for an **assortment of planets** and their orbiting **moons.**

On Earth, the natural forces of volcanoes, floods, and earthquakes combined to divide continents, raise mountains, flatten plains, and carve rivers.

Civilizations rose and fell.

Technology advanced.

Generation upon generation marched forward, writing and rewriting history. Until one day the clouds parted, everything clicked into place,

and it became
obvious to anyone
who cared to
notice ...

That a couple hundred acres of wasted swampland, prairie grass, coast line, or desert are ideal spots for

18 parcels of gently sloping hills,

sandy dunes, and verdant fairways – all of which are encircled regularly by

well-stocked beverage carts...

That a rainbow trout, grayling, steelhead, or salmon will strike madly at a well cast fly with a colorful name like Green Butt Tadpole, Parachute Royal Wulff,

Woolly Bugger,
Teeny Nymph,
Sparkle Gulper,
or Hare's Face Midge...

That the deep throated hum

and aerodynamically perfect lines
of a low-slung, high performance vehicle will inspire a
primal urge

to strike out alone for the
open road with nothing
more than a
toothbrush,
a wad of cash,
and a vague plan to
see what's over the
next mountain...

That the best songs, books, and movies are about old dogs, impossible odds,

and
the scent of
a woman's hair...

That, unless he's had an **unfortunate head injury**,

a man should never drink anything **embellished** with a

small umbrella; say anything that begins with the phrase,

"Well, that's nothing – let me
tell you about the time I...";

wear anything that "stretches to fit";

or spends any time on a
hobby where the words
"numbered, limited
edition collectibles"
are part of the common
vernacular...

That most things
worth eating
or drinking
have been

slowly **aged**,

informally

served,

and cause

mild discomfort about

three hours after
consumption . . .

That while few

experiences are more

satisfying than

*a day spent
in solitude,*

a life that is not shared is

barely worth living...

And that all of this – **the bang,** the exploding energy, the atoms, the matter, the stars,

the planets,
the global changes,
the civilizations...

...the sports, the cars, the music, the outdoor grills, the iced mugs, the dogs, the loose fitting jeans, the good advice, the cautionary tales, and all the other stuff...

all of it
is only as
important as
those who are
part of it all.

So today is the day

you are

entitled to

sit back...

Close
your
eyes...

And reflect on *your place* *in the grand scheme of things.*

Is life great

or what?